TODAY I FEEL SHY

TODAY I FEEL SHY

William L. Coleman

BETHANY HOUSE PUBLISHERS
MINNEAPOLIS, MINNESOTA 55438
A Division of Bethany Fellowship, Inc.

WILLIAM L. COLEMAN is very well known for his devotional books for young people. He is a graduate of Washington Bible College and Grace Theological Seminary. He has pastored three churches in three different states. His by-line has appeared in *Christianity Today*, *Eternity*, *Campus Life*, and several other Christian magazines. He is married, the father of three children, and currently makes his home in Nebraska.

Published by Bethany House Publishers
A Division of Bethany Fellowship, Inc.
6820 Auto Club Road, Minneapolis, MN 55438

Printed in the United States of America

Library of Congress Cataloging in Publication Data

Coleman, William L.
    Today I feel shy

    Summary: A collection of devotions designed to make you feel at ease with momentary shyness, while providing practical examples of how to overcome shy feelings.
    1. Children—Prayer books and devotions—English.
2. Bashfulness—Juvenile literature. [1. Prayer
books and devotions.   2. Bashfulness]   I. Title.

BV4870.C639 1983   248.8'2   83-9216
ISBN 0-87123-588-9 (pbk.)

Contents

A Few Guidelines

As parents we would like to guide our children away from extreme shyness. There are too many good things in life that will be missed if our children go this painful route.

Most people have a period of shyness sometime in their lives, but later recover normally. Some, however, choose it as a retreat and never lead a full life.

Often, extremes can be avoided by caring parents who help children express themselves. We cannot control a child's personality but we can furnish positive input.

This book is a tool which parents might use to help a child out of shyness. As you use it, try to keep a few guidelines in mind:

1. Children are to be heard and not just seen.
2. Do not label a child as "shy." Like most of us, they have degrees of shyness.
3. Periods of shyness are to be expected. Often children grow out of them.
4. Many people you most admire were at one time shy.
5. Quietness and shyness are not the same. Quietness chooses not to speak. Shyness is afraid to speak.

May God bless you as you continue the exciting adventure of helping your children grow.

William L. Coleman

Aurora, Nebraska

The Cat Doesn't Have Your Tongue

Has an adult
Ever teased you?
If you don't say something
Right away,
Someone might ask,
"Does the cat have your tongue?"

When I was six years old
Adults used to ask me that,
And it always made me
Feel funny.

The answer is easy.
The cat doesn't have your tongue.
But sometimes you don't feel
Like talking.

And sometimes everyone else
Is so busy talking
That it's hard
To talk anyway.

Each of us can control
His own tongue.
We tell it when
To talk
And when
To be quiet.

Some people talk
A great deal.

Some people talk
Just a little.

It's up to us
How much
We want to talk
And how much
We want to be quiet.

The cat doesn't have your tongue.
You have your own tongue.

You can stick it out
And look at it
In the mirror.

Sometimes we like
To use it.
Sometimes we let
It rest.

Nobody owns your tongue
But you.

"Self-control means controlling the tongue!" (Prov. 13:3, TLB)

You Aren't Shy

If someone says,
"You're fast,"
He doesn't mean
You are always fast.

If someone says,
"You're funny,"
He doesn't mean
You are always funny.

If someone says,
"You're resting,"
He doesn't mean
You rest all the time.

When someone says,
"You're shy,"
We might not understand.

We may think
We must be shy
All the time.

We act shy sometimes.
But that doesn't mean
We are always shy.

Can you remember a time
When you were running
After a ball
As fast as you could?

When you got to the ball
You threw it back
With all your might.

You weren't shy then.
You jumped in

And did something
As hard as you could.

Do you remember
Yelling at a ball game?
You weren't shy then.

You aren't a shy person.
Sometimes you are shy.
Sometimes you are eager
To jump in
And have a good time.

Most of us are that way.
We all change
Our feelings.

**"When a man is gloomy,
    Everything seems to go wrong;
When he is cheerful,
    Everything seems right."
(Prov. 15:15, TLB)**

A Good Handshaker

When an adult
Holds out his hand,
What do you do?

Do you back away
And turn pink?

Do you go in the kitchen
And look for your mother?

Do you stare at the floor
And refuse to look up?

Some children make an extra effort
To act grown up.
They reach out their hand
And give the adult's hand
A big shake.

Usually that makes the adult
Feel good.
And it makes the child
Feel good, too.

It's a friendly thing to do.
It's a polite thing to do.
It's a happy thing to do.

That doesn't mean you have to
Act like an adult.
You don't have to drink coffee
Or drive a car.

However, it's fun
To meet people
And to get to know them.

Try it next time.
If an adult
Puts out his hand,
Shake it strongly
And firmly,
Because you are
Growing up.

**"Shake hands warmly with each other."
(Rom. 16:16, TLB)**

Meeting Friends in Books

The world of books
Is interesting and exciting.
You get to meet so many
New people, and animals
With sleek coats
And big round eyes.

Sometimes the best part
Of a day is to sit
And look through a book
Or to have it read to you
Or to read parts by yourself.

You have heard some of
The stories so many times
That you know what will happen
Before you are finished.

Some stories are so good
That you almost feel like
You really know the characters
In the books.

It's almost as though they have
Become your friends.
And you can hardly wait
To hear more about them.

The people or animals
You meet in books
Are your friends.
They are your paper friends.
It's nice to have paper friends.

They aren't your only friends.
You have friends who live
On your block
Or in your apartment house.

You have friends who go
To your school
Or friends who go
To your church.

Paper friends are amazing
And so are real friends.
That's why we have some
Of each.

"Now you are my friends."
(John 15:15, TLB)

Look Who Likes You

Do your parents like
To talk to you
About the things you like?

Do your parents spend
Time with you
Playing games or reading
Or just sitting together?

It looks as if
They like you.

Do you have a friend
Who plays in your yard
Or who invites you
To his house?

Do you know someone
Who shares toys
With you?

It looks as if
They like you.

Do you have a grandparent
Who sends you
A birthday card?

Do you have a grandparent
Who talks to you
On the phone?

It looks as if
They like you.

Do you know that God

Knows your name
And cares about you?

Do you know that God
Has a home in heaven
For you?

It looks as if
Someone likes you.

**"For the Lord takes pleasure in his
people." (Ps. 149:4, RSV)**

Dropping Flower Pots

Sue made a mistake.
She was carrying a flower pot
For her teacher, Mrs. Jensen,
When it slipped from her hands.

The flower pot made a terrible noise
And broke in pieces.

Sue felt very badly.
And after she walked away,
A few tears filled her eyes.

All evening Sue felt badly
Until finally she went to sleep.

The next morning Sue looked sad.
When she went to school
Sue didn't want to do anything
Because she was afraid she would
Drop something.

Sue forgot that everyone drops
Something, sometime.

Sue forgot all the things
She had carried
And had not dropped.

Sue felt clumsy
And didn't trust herself.

While she was sitting
All alone
She heard a voice say,
"Sue."

It was
Mrs. Jensen's voice.

"Would you please carry
the other flower pot for me?"
Mrs. Jensen asked kindly.

"But I broke the flower pot
Yesterday," answered Sue.

"That's all right," said Mrs. Jensen.
"I have dropped things, too.
Everyone does.

"All of us make mistakes,
And when we do, we have to
Forget and try again.

"Please carry my flower pot."

Sue held her head high
And carried the flower pot
Into the next room.

"Love forgets mistakes." (Prov. 17:9, TLB)

Meeting New People

Sandy learned how to skate
From a new friend
Who moved in next door.

She enjoys meeting new people
Because she learns from them.

Sandy learned to play
Kick-the-can
From a new friend
She met at school.

She enjoys meeting new people
Because she learns from them.

A new friend gave Sandy
Her wooden spoon
With the dancing children
On the handle.

Sandy met a girl in church
Who had lived in Holland
And knew all about people from there.

She enjoys meeting new people
Because she learns from them.

And when Sandy wanted
To play with someone,
She knew many people
She could invite.

When someone new
Moved into her neighborhood
Or came to her school
Or attended her church,

Sandy tried to meet
Them right away.

Sandy has many friends
Because she doesn't
Stand back and stay
Away from people.

God has created many
Interesting and friendly people.

Sandy enjoys meeting new people
Because she learns from them.

"I was a stranger and you invited me into your home." (Matt. 25:35, TLB)

Younger Brothers and Sisters

Mary liked her younger brother,
Charlie.
Sometimes he was a pest—
But not usually.

She liked to teach
Charlie—
How to climb a tree
Or thow a ball.

Mary would sit for
A long time,
And read a picture book
To Charlie.

If Charlie wanted to ride
In the wagon,
Mary would go outside
With him.

Mary liked her younger brother,
Charlie.
Sometimes he was a pest—
But not usually.

Most of the time Mary
Was careful
How she spoke
To Charlie.

Mary knew it hurt when
People made fun of her.

So Mary tried to talk
Kindly to Charlie.

Charlie liked
Being with Mary.
You could tell
By watching him.

Mary liked her younger brother,
Charlie.
Sometimes he was a pest—
But not usually.

Mary enjoyed doing things
Without Charlie,
But she also enjoyed doing things
With Charlie.

And when she spoke to
Charlie,
Mary made Charlie feel good.

Mary liked her younger brother,
Charlie.

**"Be gentle and truly courteous to all."
(Titus 3:2, TLB)**

Answering Questions

Every once in a while
You will hear an adult
Ask a child a question.

Instead of answering
The question,
The child will blush
And try to hide.

The child might look
At the floor
Or hide behind his
Mother's leg.

When a child does that,
He is acting shy.
The child might not be shy,
But he is acting shy.

The child doesn't have
To act shy.
He or she could stand
Up straight,
Look the adult in the eye
And answer the question.

He might feel strange
Doing it the first time
Or the second time,
But soon the child
Would get used to it.

"What is your name?"
"My name is Allen."

"What do you like to do?"
"I enjoy playing trucks."

"What is your name?"
"My name is Lisa."
"What do you like to do?"
"I enjoy playing house."

It's good to learn
To answer questions.
It shows you are
Growing up.

"It is an honor to receive a frank reply." (Prov. 24:26, TLB)

A Good Loser

Have you ever seen someone
Lose a game and
Begin to cry?

Have you ever seen someone
Play dodge ball,
And when they are out
Of the game
They become angry
And shout and scream?

It's hard to lose.
When you play
You like to win
Because it's
More fun.

But you know
That when you lose
You don't have to cry;
You don't have to shout;
You don't have to yell.

The next time you play
You might win, or
You might lose again.

It's all right to lose.
You can't always catch
The ball.
You can't always win
The race.
You can't always know
The answer.
You can't always be
The first choice.

It's more fun
To play with someone
Who is a good winner and
A good loser.

That kind of person
Is fun to be around.

You are probably
The kind of person
Who can be
A good winner and
A good loser.

**"A time to get; and a time to lose."
(Eccles. 3:6, KJV)**

Toys on the Floor

Some of the best playgrounds
In the world
Are the floors in our homes.

They aren't good places
To have sandboxes
Or to play dodge ball.

They aren't good places
To run or climb
Or to make mud pies.

But the floors in our homes
Are great places to play cars
Or to build block houses
Or to change clothes on dolls.

They are excellent places
To lie on your stomach
And to read books
Or to color with crayons.

Almost before you know it
You have played on the floor
For an hour, or two,
Or three.

And when you are done playing
You know there is one more
Job to do.

Right away you pick up
Your cars, dolls, building blocks,
Or all the bottle caps,
And put them away.

It feels good
To do things
Yourself.

Doing things
Yourself
Shows you are
Growing up.

"This should be your ambition: . . . doing your own work." (1 Thess. 4:11, TLB)

Talking in Class

Your classroom must be a
Colorful place with plenty
Of pictures and drawings.

Does your classroom have chairs,
Tables and a chalkboard?

Does your classroom have a
Record player or a tape recorder?

Does your teacher sometimes
Ask questions
And the children raise
Their hands and answer?

It's fun to raise your hand
And be part of the class.

Does your teacher sometimes
Ask children
To tell stories
About their pets or
About the things
They like to do?

It's fun to raise your hand
And be part of the class.

A classroom is a good place
To talk
When the teacher asks you
To talk.

What you think is important.
What you feel is important.
What you learn is important.
What you do is important.

It's fun to raise your hand
And be part of the class.

"A time to speak up." (Eccles. 3:7, TLB)

You Have Good Sense

Are you the kind
Of person who shows
Good sense?

Good sense means the person
Stays away from danger
And tries not to get hurt.

People who try to get hurt
Do not show good sense.

Here are some ways to see
If you use good sense.
Answer each of the questions.

Do you look carefully
Before you cross the street?

Do you stop
Before you go after a ball
In the street?

Do you hold scissors correctly
Before you carry them?

Do you check the legs
On a stepladder
Before you climb up on it?

If you said yes
To all four questions,
You have been showing
Good sense.

It's important to try
New things.

It's fun to play
Games.
It's exciting to play
Adventure.

But it's very important
To be careful,
To show good sense.

People show good sense
When they are
Careful.

"Good sense is far more valuable than gold or precious jewels." (Prov. 20:15, TLB)

Are You Noisy or Quiet?

If you had to yell
As loudly as you could,
How loudly could you yell?

Could you yell loudly enough
To scare birds out of a tree?

Could you yell loudly enough
For your neighbor to hear you?

Could you yell loudly enough
To wake a sleeping cat?

If you had to yell,
You could probably yell
Very loudly.

Yelling is good when
The time is right
And when you are in
The correct place.

You are also a person
Who knows when to
Be quiet.

You know how to
Be still
And listen when
Someone else is
Talking.

Sometimes all of us
Need to be quiet
And listen.

When we listen
Carefully,
We can learn.

It's fun to learn,
Because learning
Helps us to enjoy
More things.

Yelling is good
Sometimes.
Listening is good
Sometimes.

When we listen
Carefully,
We can learn.

You are a good
Listener.

**"The wise man learns by listening."
(Prov. 21:11, TLB)**

Your Favorite Color

There is something important
About having a favorite color.
It isn't just another
Silly matter.

A favorite color is important,
Because it is *your*
Favorite color.

No one can tell you
What your favorite color is.
Only you can tell that.

And you are always right
About your favorite color.
No one can say you are wrong,
Because it is *your* favorite color.

You might change your mind
About your favorite color.
Today it might be green.
Tomorrow it might be blue.

It's all right to change
Your favorite color,
Because you can decide
For yourself.

Your favorite animal
Is important.
Your favorite book
Is important.

Your favorite coat
Is important.

You are an interesting
Person,
Because you can
Choose.

You probably can't choose
Your school.
You probably can't choose
Your bedtime.

That's all right.
That's what parents choose.

But some things
Only you
Can choose.

What is your
Favorite color—
Today?

Feeding
the Poor

At Tony's church they kept
A coffee can on a table.
There was a slit in the
Plastic top of the can.

Each week Tony dropped
Some money through the slit
In the top of the coffee can.

The money in the can
Was used to buy milk
For starving babies in
An African country.

Some weeks Tony plinked
A few pennies in the can.
Other weeks he gave
A couple of quarters.

It made Tony feel good
To help other people,
Even if they lived far away
And he probably would
Never meet them.

Tony didn't brag about it.
His family sometimes
Discussed giving.

It made Tony feel good
To help someone else.
He knew he was doing
Something important.

It feels good

To do something
Important.

Sometimes Tony would pray
For the starving babies
And ask God to help them.

Tony would thank God
That he had some money
To give to others.

It feels good
To do something
Important.

"Happy is the generous man, the one who feeds the poor." (Prov. 22:9, TLB)

Fighting for Chairs

Have you ever seen
Two children fight
For a chair?

It looks silly,
Doesn't it?

There are plenty of chairs.
Either child could go and
Get another one.

But they don't want to.
Each child wants
To get his own way.

Soon they push each other.
They pull at the chair.
They yell at each other.
And sometimes they hit.

It looks silly,
Doesn't it?

What will they do
When they grow up?
Will they fight over
Parking places or
Grocery carts?

That sounds silly,
Doesn't it?

You can be
A good person,
A strong person,
A kind person.

You never have to
Fight for a chair.

**"It is an honor for a man to stay out of a
fight." (Prov. 20:3, TLB)**

A Know-It-All

Have you met anyone
Who is a "know-it-all"?
You can't tell him anything
Because he thinks he
Already knows it.

Randy was often like that.
If someone started to show
Him how a game worked,
Randy would say, "I know,"
Before the person could
Finish his sentence.

And the worst part was
That Randy didn't know
How it worked.

When Randy tried
To play the game,
He often had trouble because
He hadn't listened.

Randy could have been
Good at many things,
But he didn't like
To be taught.

Randy thought
He was a
"Know-it-all."

As Randy grew older,
He knew a little bit
About this and
A little bit
About that.

But Randy didn't
Know much
Because Randy didn't
Like to be taught.

There are some things
We do know
And some things
We need to learn.

Smart people like
To learn
Because they will
Be able
To do more things
If they
Are willing to learn.

**"The wise man is glad to be instructed."
(Prov. 10:8, TLB)**

Talking at the Table

Do you ever have
Something inside you
That wants to get out?

All of us do sometimes.

Maybe you saw
A large airplane
Or you played
A new game.

Maybe you heard
A funny story
Or you listened to
A new song.

You have something
Inside you
And you would like
To tell it.

All of us do sometimes.

Maybe you met
A new friend.
Or you painted
A beautiful picture.

Maybe you ran
A fast race
Or you read
A new book.

You have something
Inside you

And you would like
To tell it.

All of us do sometimes.

When you sit at
The table to eat,
That would be
A good time
To tell what
Is inside you.

Your parents will want
To hear what you have
To tell.

Talking at the table
Is a good time
To tell
What is inside you.

"Whatever is in the heart overflows into speech." (Luke 6:45, TLB)

A Good Hostess

Cindy wanted to invite
Her friend Lori to her house
For the afternoon.

So Cindy began to plan
Before she called Lori.

If Lori was going to come
And if they were going to enjoy
The afternoon,
They needed to do things
They both liked.

Of course Cindy wanted
To have fun, too,
So she looked for something
Both of them would like.

Cindy had been with friends
Who did what they liked
And didn't care what
Cindy enjoyed.

That wasn't fun.

Cindy thought about it.
She collected some dolls
And gathered a few games.
She made sure they were
Things they both liked.

Cindy was being thoughtful.
Cindy was being considerate.
Cindy was being good.

Then Cindy called Lori
And they planned to
Play together.

"A man's goodness helps him all through life." (Prov. 13:6, TLB)

You Are a Magician

In some ways you are
Just like a magician.
You can make some things
Disappear.
You can make other things
Appear.

Try it, and see
What power you have.

Before you go out to play,
Tell your mother how much
You like her clothes.

Then look closely.
If she had a frown,
It probably
Disappeared,
And a wide smile
Appeared.

You must be a magician.

When you eat supper tonight
Think of one food you like;
And when you are done eating,
Tell you mother how much
You liked it.

Then look closely.
If she had a frown,
It probably
Disappeared,
And a wide smile
Appeared.

You must be a magician.

It's exciting to be able
To change people
By using a few words
At the right time.

You are such a good magician
That you can usually make
A father say, "Thank you,"
A mailman say, "Hello,"
A neighbor say, "Good morning,"
A teacher say, "I'm glad to see you."

The secret to your magic
Is easy:
Say something nice about
Someone.

Then they will usually say
Something nice to you.

"Kind words are like honey — enjoyable and healthful." (Prov. 16:24, TLB)

When You Lose a Book

Have you ever lost a book?
That's a bad feeling.
You look all over for it,
But sometimes it takes
A long time to find
A lost book.

Probably everyone has lost
A book sometime.

Maybe they lost it
For only a minute.
Maybe they lost it
For a day
Or for a whole week.

They probably looked
Under the papers,
Behind the chair,
And under the covers.

When we lose something
We look for it
As hard as we can.

But everyone loses things.
Presidents, kings, athletes,
Band leaders, plumbers,
Indian chiefs and parents lose things.

Children lose things, too.
Because children are people—
People like you.

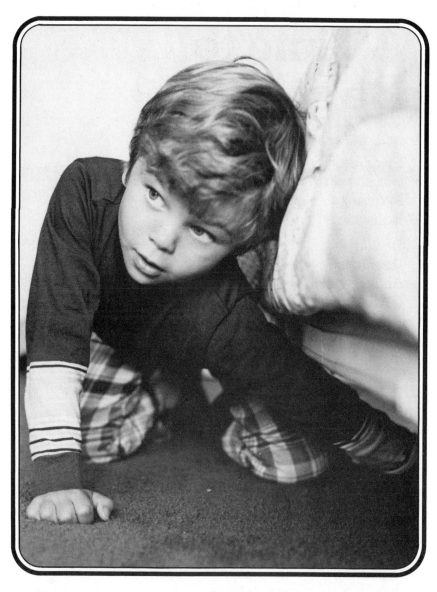

"A woman has ten valuable silver coins and loses one. Won't she light a lamp and look in every corner of the house and sweep every nook and cranny until she finds it?" (Luke 15:8, TLB)

A Time to Be Silly

What is one of your
Favorite silly things?
Do you like to
Make faces
In the mirror?

Do you like to
Wear funny clothes
And pretend to be
Grown up?

Do you like to
Stick your face
Against the window
And press your nose
Flat against it?

It's so much fun
To act silly.
We can't act silly
All the time.
But when the time
Is right,
It's so much fun
To act silly.

Even parents like
To act silly sometimes.
They know how
To make faces
And how to get on the floor
And act funny.

Sometimes parents can
Act as silly
As children.

There are some children
Who have trouble
Acting silly.

Inside, they want
To act silly,
But they hold back
And just watch.

They must miss
A lot of fun.

All of us need to
Act silly
Sometimes.

"A cheerful heart does good like medicine." (Prov. 17:22, TLB)

Getting Fussed At

Did you ever leave your shoes
On the stairs
And get scolded when your mother
Saw them?

Did you ever come home late
For dinner
And get scolded by your father
At the table?

Everybody gets into trouble
Once in a while.

All of us forget.
All of us are late.
All of us are lazy
Sometimes.

It's no fun to be
Yelled at.
Sometimes it makes you
Feel like
A little, tiny, creepy
Worm.

Of course, you aren't
A worm.
You just feel like
A worm.

It's good for us
To get scolded
Once in a while.

We learn to do better

Next time
And to be careful about what
We do.

Most of the time we do
Things right,
And nobody scolds us.

When we do get scolded,
It's all right.
We will try harder
Next time.

Most of the time
We do very well.
And we are learning
To do better.

When someone tells us
How to do better,
He is really
Helping us.

"Just as a father punishes a son he delights in to make him him better, so the Lord corrects you." (Prov. 3:12, TLB)

God Loves You

Would God love you more if
You shined your shoes every day?

Would God love you more if
You kept your bedroom neater?

Would God love you more if
You brushed your teeth every day?

There is nothing you can do
That will make God love you more.

God already loves you
Just the way you are.

But, what if you
Washed the car,
Swept the walk,
Ate vegetables and
Hugged your brother?

God already loves you
Just the way you are.

But, what if you
Did the dishes,
Emptied trash baskets,
Picked up your clothes and
Returned the game
You borrowed?

God already loves you
Just the way you are.

Those are good things,
And maybe you need
To do them.

But there is nothing

You can do
To make God
Love you more.

You can be loud
Or quiet.
You can walk fast
Or slow.
You can sing high
Or low.

God already loves you
Just the way you are.

**"I have loved you even as the Father has loved me. Live within my love."
(John 15:9, TLB)**

Say Your Name

Have you ever asked a small child
What his name is, and he
Didn't answer you?

Maybe he just turned his head
And faced the wall.
Maybe he looked at the floor
And mumbled his name
So you couldn't hear it.

Why are some children
Bashful about their name?
A name is great.
It tells who you are.

A name makes you
Different from others.
It helps tell who your
Parents are.

There is something special
About a name.
A name should be said
Brightly and clearly.

A name should never be lost
In a mumble.

You are not a number.
You are not a thing.
You are not a tree.
You are a person.

People have names,
And you have
A terrific name.

Stand straight and tall
And say your name.

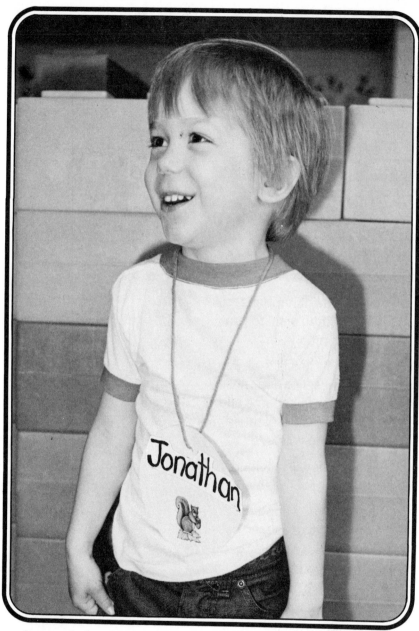

It sounds fantastic.

"If you must choose, take a good name rather than great riches." (Prov. 22:1, TLB)

When People Talk Loudly

Have you ever met an adult
Who talks very loudly?

That can be scary at first.

The grown-up is much bigger than you.
And sometimes he bends over
To get closer to you,
And his loud voice booms
Like a roaring train.

The first time it happens
Some children want to run
Away and hide.

They don't know if the adult
Is angry, upset or deaf.
Some children become afraid
Of adults because of those
Big, booming voices.

Some adults will talk loudly
No matter how they feel.

They might be happy
And glad to see you
And would love to play games
And to tell you stories.

But even when they are happy,
They still have
Big, booming voices.

Other adults use softer,
Pleasant voices.

And sometimes it's
More fun to listen to them.

An adult with a loud voice
May love you very much.

He just loves you
With a loud voice.

Someone Called You a Name

What if you could change
A person or an animal
Just by calling him by
A different name?

It could be fun.
You could call someone
A duck,
And immediately he would
Start quacking.

Or you could call a dog
A horse,
And immediately it would become
A tall dark stallion.

It could be fun,
Sometimes.
But you could hurt people.
Most people don't want to be
A duck.

Maybe that is why God
Didn't give us the power
To change people by
Calling them names.

Thank God, no one can
Change us by calling us
Names.

If someone says,
"You are stupid to do that,"
That doesn't make you stupid.

You are still you.

If someone says,
"You are clumsy,"
That doesn't make you clumsy.

You are still you.

All of us are called
A name sometime,
But that doesn't change us.

They used to call
Jesus names.
But He was still
Jesus.

And
You are still you.

**" 'You Samaritan! Foreigner! Devil!' the Jewish leaders snarled [at Jesus]."
(John 8:48, TLB)**

How Do You Sing?

There are some people
Who would like to sing,
But when the music begins,
Their mouths won't open
And their lips hardly move.

The person is singing, but
You would almost have to
Put your ear up to his mouth
In order to hear him.

The person wants to sing,
He even likes the music,
But something tries to keep
The song inside him.

Maybe he worries what
He sounds like.
Maybe he is afraid
He doesn't know
The words.

It's no fun to keep
A song inside
When the song
Is trying
To get out.

Sometimes people have to
Open up
And let the song
Out.

It's more fun

To sing.
It isn't much fun
To just sit still
And mumble.

"Let everyone bless God and sing his praises." (Ps. 66:8, TLB)

Do You Like to Tell Stories?

What is one of your
Favorite stories?
Is it about a person
Or a family?
Is it about a bear
With dark brown fur?

Do you like stories from
Large books with pictures
Or stories on television
Or stories from a Bible storybook?

Sometimes you like old stories
Read to you.
Other times you like new stories
Made up for you.

Do you ever like to tell
A story by yourself?
Have you ever told a story
To a stuffed bear
Or to a baby
Or to a young child?

Maybe you have told a story to an adult,
Maybe even to your parents.

It's fun to have everyone
Be quiet
And pay attention
While you tell a story.

Some night when
It is time to go
To bed,

You could pick out
A story
And tell it to
Your parents.

You can be a good
Storyteller,
And your parents would like
To hear you.

72

Tonight,
You be the storyteller,
Because
You are growing up.

"Jesus now told this story to his disciples."
(Luke 16:1, TLB)

It's Fun to Pretend

Linda is a smart girl.
She watches people and
Learns what they like
And don't like.

When her Uncle Bob
Comes to her house,
He always says,
"How is my bashful
Little girl?"

Linda isn't usually bashful.
But when Uncle Bob
Comes to visit,
Linda pretends to be bashful.

Linda looks at the floor,
Moves her head away
And turns a little red.

Uncle Bob seems to like it.
He takes a quarter out
Of his pocket and gives it
To "my bashful little Linda."

The rest of the time
Linda isn't bashful.
She talks to her teacher.
She talks to her neighbor.
She talks to Mr. Wilson
At the grocery store.

But when Uncle Bob
Comes to her house,
Linda becomes bashful.

It's fun to
Pretend to be bashful,
Even though she isn't,
And Linda knows
It's a game.

Trying New Things

How would you like
To ride in a spaceship,
Or to travel to the bottom
Of the ocean
In a submarine?

How would you like
To invent the first
Water fountain that gives
Orange soda—
All for free?

How would you like
To live on a ranch
And ride horses all day,
Or to own a large boat
And visit faraway islands?

Do you like to try new things?
Do you like to visit new places?
Do you like to meet new people?
Do you like to learn new stories?

Life is so interesting
Because there is so much going on.

There are forests to explore.
There are beaches to walk.
There are animals to see.
There are planes, trains, cars
And huge balloons to watch.

There are colors to put on paper,
As only you can do it.

God has created a large,
Amazing world
Filled with new things
To do and see.

It's fun to do things,
To find out what
They are like.
It's fun to try new things
And to enjoy
The world God made.

**"The intelligent man is always open to new
ideas. In fact, he looks for them."
(Prov. 18:15, TLB)**

Read to Your Parents

It's fun to
Listen to a story,
Even if you have
Heard the story before.

It's fun to look
At the pictures again
And to smile at the people
Or animals
In the story.

You like it when
Your parents
Read to you.

Sometimes your parents
Like to have you
Read to them.

If you can't read yet,
It doesn't matter.
They still like to
Have you turn the pages
And tell the story.

Sometimes your parents
Are busy
And can't listen to you
Right away.

That is all right.
All of us are
Busy sometimes.

You can ask them again,
Later.

Then you will climb up
On their laps
Or on the couch
Next to them
And show them your story.

Parents need to hear
Stories from their children,
Because children
Are very important
To their parents.

God gave children
To parents, and
God gave parents
To children.

"So give your parents joy!"
(Prov. 23:25, TLB)

Are You a Good Bouncer?

Chris could spend all day
Bouncing on a trampoline.
She had one in her backyard,
And on a sunny day
Chris bounced for hours.

Chris had learned several tricks.
She could spin in the air and
She could throw her feet out and
Bounce sitting down.

Everytime Chris went down
On the trampoline
She bounced back up
From the trampoline.

She became
Very good
At bouncing back up.

Sometimes Chris would think
About the trampoline
When she was playing ball.
If she fell down on the field,
She pretended to bounce back up.

She became
Very good
At bouncing back up.

Sometimes Chris would think
About the trampoline
When she was at school.

If she didn't do well

On a paper,
Chris thought about bouncing back,
And she did better
On the next paper.

She became
Very good
At bouncing back.

When things didn't go well
Chris didn't feel too badly,
Because she knew
She could bounce back.

**"Weeping may go on all night, but in the
morning there is joy." (Ps. 30:5, TLB)**

Your Television Friends

Who are your best friends
On television?
Are they people, cartoons
Or furry animals?

Do your television friends
Have long necks?
Do they wear red clothes or
Big purple shoes?

Television can be a good thing;
It brings interesting friends into
Your home.

You meet many television friends
Every week or every day.
You learn what they are like,
How they talk and how they walk.

When you turn the TV on
You can hardly wait
To see what your friends
Will do.

Television friends are special.
They can't do what real friends can do.
But they are still special.

Real friends can help you
Find a lost quarter.
Real friends can help you
Paint a large box.
Real friends can help you
Catch a frog.

Television friends can't
Walk around your home.
You need real friends
For that.

Television friends can't
Play ball with you.
You need real friends
For that.

But when you want
To see someone on a screen
Do things that are
Fun to watch,
Television friends are
Great friends.

"There are friends who pretend to be friends, but there is a friend who sticks closer than a brother." (Prov. 18:24, TLB)

It's Good to Be Alone

"Why don't you call Jill
And invite her over tonight?"
Peggy's mother was trying
To be helpful.

But Peggy looked at her mother,
Smiled and said, "No, thank you.'

Peggy has plenty to do,
And tonight she wants to be
All alone.

She has doll clothes to put on
Her favorite doll.
She has a picture to color.

There are a few things to put away
In her room.
She has a letter to write.

Peggy likes people, and many times
She has two or three of her friends
To her house for the evening.

They know how to laugh
And play games,
And how to giggle
For the longest time
Over nothing.

Those are people times.
But Peggy also enjoys
Her alone times.

She doesn't like to be
Alone all the time.
But Peggy doesn't want
People all the time, either.

When it was bedtime,
Peggy was tired, and
She felt good about
How much she had done.

She enjoyed sleeping
That night
And looked forward to
Seeing friends
Tomorrow.

**"And when the evening was come, he
[Jesus] was there alone."
(Matt. 14:23, KJV)**

Are You a Doctor?

Willie wasn't very old
When he found out
He was a doctor.

Willie didn't go to
Medical school.
Willie didn't have
An office.
Willie didn't give bottles
Of medicine.

But young Willie
Found out
He was a doctor.

When someone looked tired,
Or looked sad,
Or looked lonely,
Or looked worn out,
Willie would go
To work.

Willie would say
Something nice
To that person.
He would tell them
He liked their shirt or
He liked their hair or
He liked their shoes.

The person would usually
Smile at Willie
And feel better
Right away.

Doctor Willie's favorite medicine
Was kind words.
They don't cost anything,
And everybody has them.

Willie would tell people
They were
Nice,
Kind,
Good,
Fun,
Or other pleasant things.

Willie's home and school,
His church and neighborhood,
His playground and park,
Were peppered with people
He had made feel better.

Willie was a good doctor
Who gave free medicine.

"Gentle words cause life and health."
(Prov. 15:4, TLB)

Helping Others

If you stopped to think
About how many people
You have helped,
There would be too many
To remember.

How many times have you
Picked up something
And handed it to your parents?

You are the kind of person
Who helps others.

How many times have you
Shown a small child
How to use a new toy?

You are the kind of person
Who helps others.

Have you ever
Poured milk or given food
To a pet cat
Or to a pet dog
Or to a pet bird?

You felt good when you helped,
Because it is important
To help others.

You do important things,
And you are an
Important person.

When you help put food away
Or help clear the table
Or help pick up trash
In the yard,
You are doing important things.

Stand up straight and tall.
Put a smile on your face.
God has made you an
Important person.

"Greet Priscilla and Aquila my helpers in Christ Jesus." (Rom. 16:3, KJV)

Is Ricky a Bush?

Maybe Ricky didn't want
To be a child.
If he had his way
He might
Have been a bush.

It sounds silly to want
To be a bush.
But you would have
To know Ricky.

His favorite thing
In the whole world
Is to stand around
And watch other people
Have a good time.

Ricky doesn't like to
Play ball games.
Ricky doesn't like to
Climb on bars.
Ricky doesn't like to
Play tag.

Ricky really likes to
Stand around—
Like a bush.

There isn't anything wrong
With standing around
Once in a while.
But standing around
All the time
Is really boring.

Maybe Ricky would like
To play ball or

To climb on bars or
To play tag,
If he would try.

Instead,
He stands around
And is bored.

If Ricky really were
A bush,
Everything would
Be fine.

His parents could
Clip his hair
And water his feet,
And Ricky would be
A happy bush.

But Ricky isn't
A bush,
Because Ricky is
A child.

And he could learn
To join the others
And have a good time.

If you see anyone
Like this Ricky,
Invite him to join you
And not to be like a bush.

"God . . . always richly gives us all we need for our enjoyment." (1 Tim. 6:17, TLB)

Laughing at Yourself

When Kim came to the kitchen
To eat breakfast,
Everyone stopped eating
And laughed so loudly
The cat ran into
The other room.

"What's so funny?"
Kim wondered.

Her young brother, Mark,
Grabbed his mouth
So he wouldn't spit out
His food
While he laughed.

"I think it's your socks,"
Kim's mother smiled.

Kim looked down to see
A red sock and
A blue sock.

Kim started
Laughing, too.
It did look funny
To have a red sock
And a blue sock.

There was no reason
To get upset.
If Kim's mother had put on
A red sock and
A blue sock,

Kim would have laughed
At her, too.

Sometimes mistakes are funny,
Even when we make the mistakes.

Have you ever looked
In the mirror
And laughed at the way
Your hair was bunched?

Have you ever laughed
At the toothpaste
On your chin?
Have you ever laughed
At your red tongue or
At your tired eyes?

All of us look funny sometimes,
And it's nice to be able
To laugh at ourselves.

"A time to laugh." (Eccles. 3:4, TLB)

Playing Pretend

Pretending is one of the best games
Anyone has ever thought of playing.

It doesn't cost any money.
You can play pretend by yourself,
Or you can play with six people
Or more.

You can play pretend with makeup,
With wigs and with masks,
Or you can paint a paper bag
And wear it over your head.

Sometimes you get your parent's old clothes.
You wear a dress that drags on the floor
Or a coat with sleeves that cover your hands.

Usually you find a pair of shoes
That are too big,
And they bang on the floor
When you walk around.

You might pretend to be a banker,
Or a policeman, or a Congress lady,
Or a woman judge, or a housewife.

It's fun to stop being yourself
For a while.
Then it's fun to step back into
Being yourself again.

It's fun to pretend,
But it's better
To be yourself.

There are so many good things about you.
You are such an interesting person.

After you are done pretending
To be an astronaut
Or a car racer,
Your friends like to be
With you.

You are more fun
To be around
Than anyone
You could pretend
To be.

That's the way
People love you.
That's the way
God loves you—
Just the way
You are.

"Jesus said, '. . . I love you.' "
(John 13:31, 34, TLB)

Selecting Your Clothes

How do you know that
You are growing up?
You can tell because you
Are taller
Than you were last year.

You know you can't wear
The same clothes you used
To wear.

Your head comes closer to
Your parents' shoulders
Than it did.

But size isn't the only way
To tell if you are growing up.
Sometimes it isn't a good way
To tell at all.

A good way to tell if
You are growing up is to see
How many more things
You can do by yourself.

You probably brush your teeth
All by yourself.
Maybe you brush your teeth
Without being told to.

You can tell
You are growing up.

Maybe you can even
Pick out some of your clothes
By yourself.

If your mother says,
"Which dress do you
Want to wear?"
You can pick
One of them.
You make choices.

If your mother says,
"Which pair of jeans
Do you want to wear?"
You can pick
One of them.
You make choices.

Babies must have
All their decisions
Made for them.

You are growing up
And many times can
Decide for yourself.
You are using the mind
God gave you.

"There the child became a strong, robust lad, and was known for wisdom beyond his years; and God poured out his blessings on him." (Luke 2:40, TLB)

The Secret Hugger

Vonnie enjoyed making life
A game.

If there were dishes to do,
Vonnie lined them up
And pretended the dishes
Were children.

She washed each plate
In its turn and placed it
Gently in its crib.

When Vonnie wanted to
Straighten up her room,
She pretended she was
Collecting lost treasure
As she gathered clothes
And dolls from the floor.

One evening Vonnie decided
To invent a great new game.
Vonnie became the
Secret Hugger.

Quietly she tiptoed up
Behind her mother
And gently surprised her
With a hug.

Vonnie then
Sneaked around
And found her father
Reading the paper.

Carefully, Vonnie reached

Over the chair back
And hugged her father.

The Secret Hugger had
Struck again.

Vonnie's parents loved
Her new game.
Often they would hug
Vonnie in return,
And everybody would
Laugh and smile.

It's a lot of fun
To be
A Secret Hugger.

"A time to hug." (Eccles. 3:5, TLB)

Learning New Things

Kellen's first few days in school
Were hard.
School was new, and Kellen
Didn't know what to expect.

He was learning where
Everything was.
Kellen knew where
The paper and crayons were.

He could find the toy box and
The musical instruments.
Kellen knew where the box of chalk
Was kept.

But one day it was hard.
Kellen needed to go
To the bathroom,
And Kellen didn't know if there
Was a bathroom.

And if there was a bathroom,
Kellen didn't know if he was
Supposed to used it.

A school day can be long
And hard
When you need to use
The bathroom.

But Kellen didn't like to
Ask questions.
He didn't like to talk to
The teacher.

Finally Kellen went to the teacher
And asked
If they had a bathroom
At school.

Kellen felt a little silly
Afterwards.
He wondered why he had
Waited
Just to ask a question.

Questions are good,
Because they help!
Don't be afraid
To ask questions.

Your Favorite Thing to Do

If you could do
Anything you wanted,
What would you do
Today?

Would you build
A house
Out of sticks, blocks,

Dominoes or cardboard?

Would you call your friends
And set up a game
Of tag or dodge ball?

Would you go to
The park with a friend
And climb on
The monkey bars?

Would you build
A fort with a secret entrance
In your backyard?

Maybe one of your
Favorite things to do
Would be to paint pictures
With a friend.

There are so many
Good things to do,
Because God has created
An interesting world.

And God has created
An interesting you.

There are so many
Good things to do.
You will have a
Great day.

Enjoy doing some
Of your favorite things
With some of your
Favorite people.

This is a good day.

"This is the day the Lord has made. We will rejoice and be glad in it." (Ps.118:24, TLB)

Look at Their Eyes

Have you ever tried
To talk to someone
Who had a bucket
Over his head?

You probably haven't,
But if you ever did,
You probably wouldn't
Enjoy it.

While you were talking
To the person
With the bucket
Over his head,
You would wonder if
His eyes were open
Or closed,
If he was awake
Or asleep.

You wouldn't know if
The person was happy
Or sad,
If he understood
Or was confused.

When we talk to someone
Who doesn't look at us,
Who looks at the floor
Or stares out the window,
It's almost like talking
To someone who has his
Head in a bucket.

When you meet someone,
Look at his face.
And while he talks,
Look at his eyes.

It's polite to look at someone
While he is talking.
It is friendly.
It is cheerful.
It is happy.
It is growing up.

We don't have to stare
At him all the time.
That would be silly.

But when you meet someone,
And when he is talking,
It makes him feel better
If you look at his eyes.

**"The light of the eyes rejoiceth the heart."
(Prov. 15:30, KJV)**

You Aren't Bragging

If you do well
In school,
You like to tell
Your parents
About it.

If you collect some
Colorful leaves,
You like to show
Them to
Your parents.

That isn't bragging.
You are telling
Your parents
About something
You enjoyed.

Parents like to know
What things make you
Happy.

Some children don't tell
Their parents,
Because they think that
Is bragging.

Telling your parents
Is sharing,
And sharing
Is good for all
Of us.

What did you do today?

What did you enjoy?
What was interesting?
What was fun?
What was hard?
What was happy?

Parents would like to know
About the things
You do.

When Is Your Birthday?

How do you celebrate
Your birthday?
Do you have a cake
With candles?
Do you get a present
Or two?

Do you celebrate
Your birthday
With your family,
Or do you invite
A few people
And have a party?

Birthday parties are fun,
Because people are happy—
Happy you are a year older
And are growing up.

The people at the party think,
"We are glad you are here.
You have been on earth for
Five years, seven years, nine years or more,
And it's great having you here."

You are special to the people
At your birthday party.
They are smiling, laughing,
Having a good time
Because you are here.

They have been able
To enjoy you
For another full year.

Having you around
Makes them feel good.

Birthdays are special
Because you are special.

Have a terrific birthday
Again this year.

"Time went by and the child grew and was weaned; and Abraham gave a party to celebrate the happy occasion." (Gen. 21:8, TLB)

The Forgotten Truck

Pete was playing
In the sandbox
In his backyard.

He was digging
A *very* deep tunnel.
Suddenly his shovel
Bumped against something hard.
He reached into the hole
And pulled out
His favorite toy truck!

It was a small, metal
Dump truck.
It used to be red and yellow,
But now almost all
The color was gone.
And one little rubber wheel
Was missing.

But Pete loved that truck.
It fit just right
In the palm of his hand.
And he could take it
Any place he went
Because it fit
In his pocket.

Pete was so thankful
He had found his
Favorite truck.

Pete seemed to be

Thankful
For most things.

He was thankful for
The place to play ball
In his backyard.

He was thankful for
The set of trucks
His Uncle Fred
Had given him.

Pete was thankful
For parents
Who loved him.

Sometimes Pete would
Smile from ear to ear
Because he felt
So thankful.

Sometimes Pete would
Talk to God
Because he felt
So thankful.

**"Oh, thank the Lord, for he's so good."
(Ps. 118:1, TLB)**

Asking Questions

Why do kites have tails?
Why are birds different colors?
Where does paint come from?
How does a street light come on
When it gets dark?

You probably have lots
Of questions.
Sometimes you ask
The questions
And sometimes
You don't.

What will you look like
When you grow up?
Will your hair color change?
Will you be tall or short?
Will you be left-handed
Or right-handed?

You probably have
Many questions.
Sometimes you ask
The questions
And sometimes
You don't.

What happens when
You go to sleep?
Do you stop breathing?
Do your eyes open when
You are dreaming?

Do your parents come
Into the room
While you are asleep?

You probably have lots
Of questions.
Sometimes you ask
The questions
And sometimes
You don't.

Which is faster,
A bird or a plane?
How high can
You throw a stone?
How deep is the ocean?

Some questions are
About things.
Some questions are
About people.
Some questions are
About yourself.

It's good to ask questions.
That is how we learn
More about our world.
It is also how we learn
More about ourselves.

When Jesus was a child,
He loved to ask questions.
It helped Him learn, too.

"He was in the Temple, sitting among the teachers of Law, discussing deep questions with them." (Luke 2:46, TLB)

Stories We Don't Like

Angie likes to hear
Stories about herself.
Her mother tells her
About the time Angie
Was chased by a goat
At her grandfather's farm.

Angie likes the story
Because it's funny.

She also likes the story
About the time when she
Found a five-dollar bill
At the grocery store
And gave it back to
The lady who dropped it.

Those stories make Angie
Feel good and laugh.

But there is one story
That Angie doesn't like.

Her mother told the story
About the time Angie
Dropped three dozen eggs
On the kitchen floor
And broke nearly all of them.

When her mother told that story
Angie's Uncle Ed laughed and said,
"Poor Angie, she can't carry
Anything."

Her mother liked the story.
Uncle Ed liked the story.
But it make Angie
Feel badly.

One day Angie told
Her mother
Why she didn't like
The story.

Her mother was surprised
And promised
Never to tell the story
Again.

Angie's mother hadn't known
She was hurting Angie's feelings.

Angie was smart to tell
Her mother.

Most of us know stories
We don't like to hear.

"Some people like to make cutting remarks, but the words of the wise soothe and heal." (Prov. 12:18, TLB)

S-h-h-h!
Don't Talk

Sometimes you feel like
Being quiet.
You don't have to talk
All the time.

You aren't shy;
You aren't unhappy;
You aren't afraid.

Sometimes you feel like
Being quiet.

It would be terrible
If you had to talk
All the time.

Your jaws would
Get tired.
Your head might hurt
From hearing
Yourself all day.

You aren't shy;
You aren't unhappy;
You aren't afraid.

Sometimes you feel like
Being quiet.

And when you are done
Being quiet,
You can talk
Again.

But for now you would
Like to stop talking.

You aren't shy;
You aren't unhappy;
You aren't afraid.

Sometimes you feel like
Being quiet.

"A time to be quiet." (Eccles. 3:7)

Other Books in this Series by the Same Author

My Hospital Book
*Getting Ready for My First Day
    of School*
The Good Night Book
The Sleep Tight Book
Today I Feel Like a Warm Fuzzy
Today I Feel Loved